1984 PULITZER PRIZE FOR DRAMA

Glengarry Glen Ross

A PLAY

by David Mamet

SAMUEL FRENCH, INC.

45 WEST 25TH STREET   NEW YORK 10010

7623 SUNSET BOULEVARD   HOLLYWOOD 90046

LONDON   *TORONTO*

GLENGARRY GLEN ROSS was first presented at The Cottlesloe Theatre, London, England, on September 21, 1983 with the following cast:

```
SHELLY LEVENE ................................ Derek Newark
JOHN WILLIAMSON .............................. Karl Johnson
DAVE MOSS ...................................... Trevor Ray
GEORGE ARONOW ................................ James Grant
RICHARD ROMA ................................ Jack Shepherd
JAMES LINGK ................................. Tony Haygarth
BAYLEN ........................................ John Tams
```
Directed by Bill Bryden

The U.S. premiere of the play took place at The Goodman Theatre of the Arts Institute of Chicago in a Chicago Theatre Groups, Inc. production on February 6, 1984 with the following cast:

```
SHELLY LEVENE ............................... Robert Prosky
JOHN WILLIAMSON ................................. J.T. Walsh
DAVE MOSS ................................... James Tolkan
GEORGE ARONOW ............................. Mike Nussbaum
RICHARD ROMA ............................... Joe Mantegna
JAMES LINGK ............................ William L. Peterson
BAYLEN ...................................... Jack Wallace
```
Directed by Gregory Mosher

GLENGARRY GLEN ROSS opened on Broadway at the John Golden Theatre March 25, 1984, presented by Elliot Martin, the Shubert Organization, Arnold Berhard and the Goodman Theatre. The cast was as follows:

```
SHELLY LEVENE ............................... Robert Prosky
JOHN WILLIAMSON ................................. J.T. Walsh
DAVE MOSS ................................... James Tolkan
GEORGE ARONOW ............................. Mike Nussbaum
RICHARD ROMA ............................... Joe Mantegna
JAMES LINGK ................................... Lane Smith
BAYLEN ...................................... Jack Wallace
```

```
Director .................................... Gregory Mosher
Lighting ...................................... Kevin Rigdon
Costumes ....................................... Nan Cibula
Sets ........................................ Michael Merritt
```

This play is dedicated to
Harold Pinter

THE CHARACTERS

WILLIAMSON, BAYLEN, ROMA, LINGK — Men in their early forties.

LEVENE, MOSS, AARONOW — Men in their fifties.

THE SCENE

The three scenes of Act One take place in a Chinese restaurant.

Act Two takes place in a real estate office.

Glengarry Glen Ross

ACT ONE

SCENE 1

A booth at a Chinese restaurant, WILLIAMSON and LEVENE are seated at the booth.

LEVENE. John . . . John . . . John. Okay. John. John. Look: (*pause*) The Glengarry Highland's leads, you're sending Roma out. Fine. He's a good man. We know what he is. He's fine. All I'm saying, you look at the *board*, he's throwing . . . wait, wait, wait, he's throwing them *away*, he's throwing the leads away. All that I'm saying, that you're wasting leads. I don't want to tell you your *job*. All that I'm saying, things get *set*, I know they do, you get a certain *mindset*. . . . A guy gets a reputation. We know how this . . . all I'm saying, put a *closer* on the job. There's more than one man for the . . . Put a . . . wait a second, put a *proven man out* . . . and you watch, now *wait* a second—and you watch your *dollar* volumes. . . . You start closing them for *fifty* 'stead of *twenty-five* . . . you put a *closer* on the . . .

WILLIAMSON. Shelly, you blew the last . . .

LEVENE. No. John. No. Let's wait, let's back up here, I did . . . will you please? Wait a second. Please. I didn't "blow" them. No. I didn't "blow" them. No. One kicked *out*, one I closed . . .

WILLIAMSON. . . . you didn't close . . .

LEVENE. . . . I, if you'd *listen* to me. Please. I *closed* the cocksucker. His *ex*, John, his *ex*, *I* didn't know he was married . . . he, the *judge* invalidated the . . .

WILLIAMSON. Shelly.

LEVENE. . . . and what is that, John? What? Bad *luck*.

7

That's all it is. I pray in your *life* you will never find it runs in streaks. That's what it does, that's all it's doing. Streaks. I pray it misses you. That's all I want to say.

WILLIAMSON. (*pause*) What about the other two?

LEVENE. What two?

WILLIAMSON. Four. You had four leads. One kicked out, one the *judge*, you say . . .

LEVENE. . . . you want to see the court records? John? Eh? You want to go down . . .

WILLIAMSON. . . . no . . .

LEVENE. . . . do you want to go down*town* . . . ?

WILLIAMSON. . . . no . . .

LEVENE. . . . then . . .

WILLIAMSON. . . . I only . . .

LEVENE. . . . then what is this "you *say*" shit, what is that? (*pause*) What is that . . . ?

WILLIAMSON. All that I'm saying . . .

LEVENE. What is this "you *say*"? A deal kicks out . . . I got to *eat*. *Shit*, Williamson, *shit*. You . . . Moss . . . Roma . . . look at the *sheets* . . . look at the *sheets*. Nineteen *eighty,* eighty-*one* . . . eighty-*two* . . . six months of eighty-two . . . who's there? Who's up there?

WILLIAMSON. Roma.

LEVENE. Under him?

WILLIAMSON. Moss.

LEVENE. Bull*shit*. John. Bull*shit*. April, September 1981. It's *me*. It isn't fucking *Moss*. Due respect, he's an *order* taker, John. He *talks*, he talks a good game, look at the *board*, and it's *me*, John, it's me . . .

WILLIAMSON. Not lately it isn't.

LEVENE. Lately kiss my ass lately. That isn't how you build an org . . . talk, talk to Murray. Talk to Mitch. When we were on Peterson, who paid for his fucking *car*? You talk to him. The *Seville* . . . ? He came in, "You bought that for me Shelly." Out of *what*? Cold *calling. Nothing.* Sixty-*five*, when we were there, with Glen *Ross* Farms? You call 'em downtown. What was that? *Luck*? That was "luck"? *Bull*shit, John. You're burning my ass, I can't get a fucking *lead* . . . you think that was luck. My stats for those years? Bull*shit* . . . over that period of time . . . ? Bull*shit*. It wasn't luck. It was *skill*. You want to throw that away, John . . . ? You want to throw that away?

WILLIAMSON. It isn't me . . .

LEVENE. . . . it isn't you . . . ? Who *is* it? Who is this I'm talking to? I need the *leads* . . .

WILLIAMSON. . . . after the thirtieth . . .

LEVENE. Bull*shit* the thirtieth, I don't get on the board the thirtieth, they're going to can my ass. I need the leads. I need them now. Or I'm gone, and you're going to miss me, John, I swear to you.

WILLIAMSON. Murray . . .

LEVENE. . . . you *talk* to Murray . . .

WILLIAMSON. I have. And my job is to marshal those leads . . .

LEVENE. Marshal the leads . . . marshal the leads? What the fuck, what bus did *you* get off of, we're here to fucking *sell*. *Fuck* marshaling the leads. What the fuck talk is that? What the fuck talk is that? Where did you learn that? In school? (*pause*) That's "talk," my friend, that's "talk." Our job is to *sell*. I'm the *man* to sell. I'm getting garbage. (*pause*) You're giving it to me, and what I'm saying is it's *fucked*.

WILLIAMSON. You're saying that I'm fucked.

LEVENE. Yes. (*pause*) I am. I'm sorry to antagonize you.

WILLIAMSON. Let me . . .

LEVENE. . . . and I'm going to get bounced and you're
. . .

WILLIAMSON. . . . let me . . . are you listening to
me . . . ?

LEVENE. Yes.

WILLIAMSON. Let me tell you something, Shelly. I do
what I'm hired to do. I'm . . . wait a second. I'm *hired*
watch the leads. I'm given . . . hold on, I'm given a
policy. My job is to *do that.* What I'm *told.* That's it.
You, wait a second, *anybody* falls below a certain mark
I'm not *permitted* to give them the premium leads.

LEVENE. Then how do they come up above that
mark? With *dreck* . . . ? That's *nonsense.* Explain this to
me. 'Cause it's a waste, and it's a stupid waste. I want to
tell you something . . .

WILLIAMSON. You know what those leads cost?

LEVENE. The premium leads. Yes. I know what they
cost. John. Because I, *I* generated the dollar revenue
sufficient to *buy* them. Nineteen senny-*nine*, you know
what I made? Senny-*nine*? Ninety-six thousand dollars.
John? For *Murray* . . . For *Mitch* . . . look at the sheets
. . .

WILLIAMSON. Murray said . . .

LEVENE. *Fuck* him. *Fuck* Murray. John? You know?
You tell him I said so. What does *he* fucking know?
He's going to have a "sales" contest . . . you know what
our sales contest used to be? *Money.* A *fortune.* Money
lying on the ground. Murray? When was the last time *he*
went out on a sit? Sales contest? It's *laughable.* It's cold
out there now, John. It's tight. Money is *tight.* This ain't
sixty-five. It ain't. It just ain't. See? See? Now, I'm a
good *man*—but I need a . . .

WILLIAMSON. Murray said . . .

LEVENE. John. John. . . .

WILLIAMSON. Will you please wait a second. Shelly. Please. Murray told me: the hot leads . . .

LEVENE. . . . ah, *fuck* this . . .

WILLIAMSON. The . . . Shelly? (*pause*) The hot leads are assigned according to the board. During the contest. *Period*. Anyone who beats fifty per . . .

LEVENE. That's fucked. That's fucked. You don't look at the fucking *percentage*. You look at the *gross*.

WILLIAMSON. Either way. You're out.

LEVENE. I'm out.

WILLIAMSON. Yes.

LEVENE. I'll tell you why I'm out. I'm *out*, you're giving me toilet paper. John, I've *seen* those leads. I saw them when I was at Homestead, we pitched those cocksuckers Rio Rancho nineteen sixty-*nine* they wouldn't buy. They couldn't buy a fucking *toaster*. They're *broke*, John. They're cold. They're deadbeats, you can't judge on that. Even so. Even so. Alright. Fine. Fine. Even so. I go in, FOUR FUCKING LEADS they got their money in a *sock*. They're fucking *Polacks*, John. Four leads. I close two. *Two*. Fifty per . . .

WILLIAMSON. . . . they kicked out.

LEVENE. They *all* kick out. You run in *streaks*, pal. *Streaks*. I'm . . . I'm . . . don't look at the *board*, look at *me*. Shelly Levene. *Anyone*. *Ask* them on Western. Ask Getz at Homestead. Go ask Jerry Graff. You know who I am . . . I NEED A SHOT. I got to get on the fucking board. Ask them. *Ask* them. Ask them who ever picked up a check I was flush. Moss, Jerry Graff, Mitch himself . . . Those guys *lived* on the business I brought in. They *lived* on it . . . and so did Murray, John. You were here you'd of benefited from it too. And now I'm saying this. Do I want charity? Do I want *pity*? I want *sits*. I want leads don't come right out of a *phone book*. Give me a lead hotter than that, I'll go in and close it. Give me a chance. That's all I want. I'm going to *get* up on that fucking board and all I want is a chance. It's a *streak* and I'm going to turn it around. (*pause*) I need your help. (*pause*)

WILLIAMSON. I can't do it, Shelly. (*pause*)

LEVENE. Why?

WILLIAMSON. The leads are assigned randomly . . .

LEVENE. *Bullshit*, *bullshit*, you assign them. . . . What are you *telling* me?

WILLIAMSON. . . . apart from the top men on the contest board.

LEVENE. Then put me on the board.

WILLIAMSON. You start closing again, you'll *be* on the board.

LEVENE. I can't close these leads, John. No one can. It's a joke. John, look, just give me a hot lead. Just give me two of the premium leads. As a "test," alright? As a "test" and I promise you . . .

WILLIAMSON. I can't do it, Shel. (*pause*)

LEVENE. I'll give you ten percent. (*pause*)

WILLIAMSON. Of what?

LEVENE. Of my end what I close.

WILLIAMSON. And what if you don't close.

LEVENE. I *will* close.

WILLIAMSON. What if you *don't* close . . . ?

LEVENE. I *will* close.

WILLIAMSON. What if you *don't*? Then *I'm* fucked. You see . . . ? Then it's *my* job. That's what I'm *telling* you.

LEVENE. I *will* close. John, John, ten percent. I can get hot. You *know* that . . .

WILLIAMSON. Not lately you can't . . .

LEVENE. Fuck that. That's defeatist. Fuck that. Fuck it. . . . Get on my side. *Go* with me. Let's *do* something. You want to run this office, *run* it.

WILLIAMSON, Twenty percent. (*pause*)

LEVENE. Alright.

WILLIAMSON. And fifty bucks a lead.

LEVENE. John. (*pause*) Listen. I want to talk to you. Permit me to do this a second. I'm older than you. A man acquires a reputation. On the street. What he does when he's *up*, what he does otherwise. . . . I said "ten," you said "no." You said "twenty." I said "fine," I'm not going to fuck with you, how can I beat that, you tell me? . . . Okay. Okay. We'll . . . Okay. Fine. We'll . . . Alright, twenty percent, and fifty bucks a lead. That's fine. For now. That's fine. A month or two we'll talk. A month from now. Next month. After the thirtieth. (*pause*) We'll talk.

WILLIAMSON. What are we going to say?

LEVENE. No. You're right. That's for later. We'll talk in a month. What have you got? I want two sits. Tonight.

WILLIAMSON. I'm not sure I have two.

LEVENE. I saw the board. You've got *four* . . .

WILLIAMSON. I've got *Roma*. Then I've got Moss . . .

LEVENE. *Bullshit.* They ain't been in the office yet. Give 'em some stiff. We have a deal or not? Eh? Two sits. The Des Plaines. Both of 'em, six and ten, you can do it . . . six and ten . . . eight and eleven, I don't give a shit, you set 'em up? Alright? The two sits in Des Plaines.

WILLIAMSON. Alright.

LEVENE. Good. Now we're talking. (*pause*)

WILLIAMSON. A hundred bucks. (*pause*)

LEVENE. Now? (*pause*) *Now*?

WILLIAMSON. Now. (*pause*) *Yes . . . When*?

LEVENE. Ah, *shit*, John. (*pause*)

WILLIAMSON. I wish I could.

LEVENE. You fucking asshole. (*pause*) I haven't got it. (*pause*) I haven't got it, John. (*pause*) I'll pay you tomorrow. (*pause*) I'm coming in here with the sales, I'll pay you *tomorrow. (pause)* I haven't *got* it, when I pay, the *gas* . . . I get back the hotel, I'll bring it in tomorrow.

WILLIAMSON. Can't do it.

LEVENE. I'll give you thirty on them now, I'll bring the rest tomorrow. I've got it at the hotel. (*pause*) John? (*pause*) We do that, for chrissake?

WILLIAMSON. No.

LEVENE. I'm asking you. As a favor to me? (*pause*) John. (*long pause*) John: my *daughter* . . .

WILLIAMSON. I can't do it, Shelly.

LEVENE. Well, I want to tell you something, fella, wasn't long I could pick up the phone, call *Murray* and I'd have your job. You know that? Not too *long* ago. For what? For *nothing.* "Mur, this new kid burns my ass." "Shelly, he's out." You're gone before I'm back from lunch. I bought him a trip to Bermuda once . . .

WILLIAMSON. I have to go . . . (*gets up*)

LEVENE. Wait. Alright. Fine. (*starts going in pocket for money*) The one. Give me the lead. Give me the one lead. The best one you have.

WILLIAMSON. I can't split them. (*pause*)

LEVENE. Why?

WILLIAMSON. Because I say so.

LEVENE. (*pause*) Is that it? Is that *it*? You want to do business that way . . . ? (*WILLIAMSON gets up, leaves money on the table.*) You want to do business that way . . . ? Alright. Alright. Alright. Alright. What is there on the other list . . . ?

WILLIAMSON. You want something off the B list?

LEVENE. *Yeah.* Yeah.

WILLIAMSON. Is that what you're saying?

LEVENE. That's what I'm saying. Yeah. (*pause*) I'd like something off the other list. Which, very least, that I'm entitled to. If I'm still *working* here, which for the moment I guess that I am. (*pause*) What? I'm sorry I spoke harshly to you.

WILLIAMSON. That's alright.

LEVENE. The deal still stands, our other thing. (*WILLIAMSON shrugs. Starts out of the booth.*) Good. Mmm. I, you know, I left my wallet back at the hotel.

SCENE 2

A booth at the restaurant. MOSS and AARONOW seated. After the meal.

Moss. Polacks and deadbeats.

AARONOW. ... Polacks ...

Moss. Deadbeats *all.*

AARONOW. ... they hold on to their money ...

Moss. All of 'em. They, *hey*: it happens to us all.

AARONOW. Where am I going to work?

Moss. You have to cheer up, George, you aren't out yet.

AARONOW. I'm not?

Moss. You missed a fucking sale. Big deal. A deadbeat Polack. Big deal. How you going to sell 'em in the *first* place ... ? Your mistake, you shoun'a took the lead.

AARONOW. I had to.

Moss. You had to, yeah. Why?

AARONOW. To get on the . . .

Moss. To get on the board. Yeah. How you goan'a get on the board sell'n a Polack? And I'll tell you, I'll tell you what *else*. You listening? I'll tell you what else: don't ever try to sell an Indian.

AARONOW. I'd never try to sell an Indian.

Moss. You get those names come up, you ever get 'em, "Patel"?

AARONOW. Mmm . . .

Moss. You ever get 'em?

AARONOW. Well I think I had one once.

Moss. You did?

AARONOW. I . . . I don't know.

Moss. You had one you'd know it. *Patel*. They keep coming up. I don't know. They like to talk to salesmen. (*pause*) They're *lonely*, something. (*pause*) They like to feel *superior*, I don't know. Never bought a fucking thing. You're sitting down "The Rio Rancho *this*, the blah blah blah," "The Mountain View—" "Oh yes. My brother told me that. . . ." They got a grapevine. Fuckin' Indians, George. Not my cup of tea. Speaking of which I want to tell you something (*pause*) I never got a cup of tea with them. You see them in the restaurants. A supercilious race. What is this *look* on their face all the time? I don't know. (*pause*) I don't know. Their broads all look like they just got fucked with a dead *cat*, *I* don't know. (*pause*) I don't know. I don't like it. Christ . . .

AARONOW. What?

Moss. The whole fuckin' thing . . . The pressure's just too great. You're ab . . . you're absolu . . . they're too important. All of them. You go in the door. I . . . "I got to *close* this fucker, or I don't eat lunch," "or I don't win the *Cadillac*. . . ." We fuckin' work too hard. You work

too hard. We all, I remember when we were at Platt . . .
huh? Glen Ross Farms . . . *didn't* we sell a bunch of
that . . . ?

AARONOW. They came in and they, you know . . .

Moss. Well, they fucked it up.

AARONOW. They did.

Moss. They killed the goose.

AARONOW. They did.

Moss. And now . . .

AARONOW. We're stuck with *this* . . .

Moss. We're stuck with *this* fucking shit . . .

AARONOW. . . . *this* shit . . .

Moss. It's too . . .

AARONOW. It is.

Moss. Eh?

AARONOW. It's too . . .

Moss. You get a bad month, all of a . . .

AARONOW. You're on this . . .

Moss. All of, they got you on this "board . . ."

AARONOW. I, I . . . I . . .

Moss. Some *contest* board . . .

AARONOW. I . . .

Moss. It's not right.

AARONOW. It's not.

Moss. No. (*pause*)

AARONOW. And it's not right to the *customers*.

Moss. I know it's not. I'll tell you, you got, you know,
you got . . . what did I learn as a kid on Western? Don't
sell a guy one car. Sell him *five* cars over fifteen years.

AARONOW. That's right.

Moss. Eh . . . ?

AARONOW. That's right.

Moss. Goddamn right, that's right. Guys come on:

"Oh, the blah blah blah, *I* know what I'll do: I'll go in and rob everyone blind and go to Argentina cause nobody ever *thought* of this before."

AARONOW. . . . that's right . . .

Moss. Eh?

AARONOW. No. That's absolutely right.

Moss. And so they kill the goose . . . and, and a fuckin' *man*, worked all his *life* has got to . . .

AARONOW. . . . that's right . . .

Moss. . . . cower in his boots . . .

AARONOW. (*simultaneously with "boots"*) Shoes, boots, yes . . .

Moss. For some fuckin' "Sell ten thousand and you win the steak knives . . ."

AARONOW. For some *sales* pro . . .

Moss. . . . sale promotion, "You *lose*, then we fire your . . ." No. It's *medieval* . . . it's wrong. "Or we're going to fire your ass." It's wrong.

AARONOW. Yes.

Moss. Yes, it is. And you know who's responsible?

AARONOW. Who?

Moss. You know who it is. It's Mitch. And Murray. 'Cause it doesn't have to be this way.

AARONOW. No.

Moss. Look at Jerry Graff. He's *clean*, he's doing business for *himself*, he's got his, that *list* of his with the *nurses* . . . see? You see? That's *thinking*. Why take ten percent? A ten percent comm . . . why are we giving the rest away? What are we giving ninety per . . . for *nothing*. For some jerk sit in the office tell you "Get out there and close." "Go win the Cadillac." Graff. He goes out and *buys*. He pays top dollar for the . . . you see?

AARONOW. Yes.

Moss. That's *thinking*. Now, he's got the leads, he

goes in business for *himself*. He's . . . that's what I . . . that's *thinking*! "Who? Who's got a steady *job*, a couple bucks nobody's touched, who?"

AARONOW. Nurses.

Moss. So Graff buys a fucking list of nurses, one grand—if he paid two I'll eat my hat—four, five thousand nurses, and he's going *wild* . . .

AARONOW. He is?

Moss. He's doing *very* well.

AARONOW. I heard that they were running cold.

Moss. The nurses?

AARONOW. Yes.

Moss. You hear a *lot* of things. . . . He's doing very well. He's doing *very* well.

AARONOW. With River Oaks?

Moss. River Oaks, Brook Farms. *All* of that shit. Somebody told me, you know what he's clearing *himself*? Fourteen, fifteen grand a *week*.

AARONOW. Himself?

Moss. That's what I'm *saying*. Why? The *leads*. He's got the good leads . . . what are we, we're sitting in the shit here. Why? We have to go to *them* to *get* them. Huh. Ninety percent our sale, we're *paying* to the *office* for the *leads*.

AARONOW. The leads, the overhead, the telephones, there's *lots* of things.

Moss. What do you need? A *telephone*, some broad to say "Good morning," nothing . . . nothing . . .

AARONOW. No, it's not that simple, Dave . . .

Moss. *Yes*. It *is*. It *is* simple, and you know what the hard part is?

AARONOW. What?

Moss. Starting up.

AARONOW. What hard part?

Moss. Of doing the thing. The dif . . . the difference. Between me and Jerry Graff. Going to business for yourself. The hard part is . . . you know what it is?

Aaronow. What?

Moss. Just the *act*.

Aaronow. What act?

Moss. To say "I'm going on my own." 'Cause what you do, George, let me tell you what you do: you find yourself in *thrall* to someone else. And we *enslave* ourselves. To *please*. To win some fucking *toaster* . . . to . . . to . . . and the guy who got there first made *up* those . . .

Aaronow. That's right . . .

Moss. He made *up* those rules, and we're working for *him*.

Aaronow. That's the truth . . .

Moss. That's the *God's* truth. And it gets me depressed. I *swear* that it does. At MY AGE. To see a goddamn: "Somebody wins the Cadillac this month. P.S. Two guys get fucked."

Aaronow. *Huh.*

Moss. You don't *ax* your sales force.

Aaronow. No.

Moss. You . . .

Aaronow. You . . .

Moss. You *build* it!

Aaronow. That's what I . . .

Moss. You fucking *build* it! Men come . . .

Aaronow. Men come *work* for you . . .

Moss. . . . you're absolutely right.

Aaronow. They . . .

Moss. They have . . .

Aaronow. When they . . .

Moss. Look look look look, when they *build* your

business, then you can't fucking turn around, *enslave* them, treat them like *children*, fuck them up the ass, leave them to fend for themselves . . . no. (*pause*) No. (*pause*) You're absolutely right, and I want to tell you something.

AARONOW. What?

Moss. I want to tell you what somebody should do.

AARONOW. What?

Moss. Someone should stand up and strike *back*.

AARONOW. What do you mean?

Moss. *Somebody* . . .

AARONOW. Yes . . . ?

Moss. Should do something to *them*.

AARONOW. What?

Moss. Something. To pay them back. (*pause*) Someone, someone should hurt them. Murray and Mitch.

AARONOW. Someone should hurt them.

Moss. Yes.

AARONOW. (*pause*) How?

Moss. How? Do something to hurt them. Where they live.

AARONOW. What? (*pause*)

Moss. Someone should rob the office.

AARONOW. Huh.

Moss. That's what I'm *saying*. We were, if we were that kind of guys, to knock it off, and *trash* the joint, it looks like robbery, and *take* the fuckin' leads out of the files . . . go to Jerry Graff. (*long pause*)

AARONOW. What could somebody get for them?

Moss. What could we *get* for them? I don't know. Buck a *throw* . . . buck-a-half a throw . . . I don't know. . . . Hey, who knows what they're worth, what do they *pay* for them? All told . . . must be, I'd . . . three bucks a throw . . . *I* don't know.

AARONOW. How many leads have we got?

Moss. The *Glengarry* . . . the premium leads . . . ? I'd say we got five thousand. Five. Five thousand leads.

AARONOW. And you're saying a fella could take and sell these leads to Jerry Graff.

Moss. Yes.

AARONOW. How do you know he'd buy them?

Moss. Graff? Because I worked for him.

AARONOW. You haven't talked to him.

Moss. No. What do you mean? Have I talked to him about *this*? (*pause*)

AARONOW. Yes. I mean are you actually *talking* about this, or are we just . . .

Moss. No, we're just . . .

AARONOW. We're just "*talking*" about it.

Moss. We're just *speaking* about it. (*pause*) As an *idea*.

AARONOW. As an idea.

Moss. Yes.

AARONOW. We're not actually *talking* about it.

Moss. No.

AARONOW. Talking about it as a . . .

Moss. *No.*

AARONOW. As a *robbery*.

Moss. As a "robbery"?! No.

AARONOW. *Well*. Well . . .

Moss. *Hey*. (*pause*)

AARONOW. So all this, um, you didn't, actually, you didn't actually go talk to Graff.

Moss. Not actually, no. (*pause*)

AARONOW. You didn't?

Moss. No. Not actually.

AARONOW. Did you?

Moss. What did I say?

AARONOW. What did you say?

Moss. Yes. (*pause*) I said, "Not actually." The fuck *you* care, George? We're just *talking* . . .

AARONOW. We are?

Moss. Yes. (*pause*)

AARONOW. Because, because, you know, it's a *crime.*

Moss. That's right. It's a crime. It is a crime. It's also very safe.

AARONOW. You're actually *talking* about this?

Moss. That's right. (*pause*)

AARONOW. You're going to steal the leads?

Moss. Have I said that? (*pause*)

AARONOW. Are you? (*pause*)

Moss. Did I say that?

AARONOW. Did you talk to Graff?

Moss. Is that what I said?

AARONOW. What did he say?

Moss. What did he say? He'd *buy* them. (*pause*)

AARONOW. You're going to steal the leads and sell the leads to him? (*pause*)

Moss. Yes.

AARONOW. What will he pay?

Moss. A buck a shot.

AARONOW. For five thousand?

Moss. However they are, that's the deal. A buck a throw. Five thousand dollars. Split it half and half.

AARONOW. You're saying "me."

Moss. Yes. (*pause*) Twenty-five hundred apiece. One night's work, and the job with Graff. Working the premium leads. (*pause*)

AARONOW. A job with Graff.

Moss. Is that what I said?

AARONOW. He'd give me a job.

Moss. He would take you on. Yes. (*pause*)

AARONOW. Is that the truth?

Moss. Yes. It is, George. (*pause*) Yes. It's a big decision. (*pause*) And it's a big reward. (*pause*) It's a big reward. For one night's work. (*pause*) But it's got to be tonight.

AARONOW. What?

Moss. What? What? The *leads*.

AARONOW. You have to steal the leads tonight?

Moss. That's *right*, the guys are moving them downtown. After the thirtieth. Murray and Mitch. After the contest.

AARONOW. You're, you're saying so you have to go in there tonight and . . .

Moss. *You* . . .

AARONOW. I'm sorry?

Moss. *You.* (*pause*)

AARONOW. Me?

Moss. *You* have to go in. (*pause*) *You* have to get the leads. (*pause*)

AARONOW. I do?

Moss. Yes.

AARONOW. I . . .

Moss. It's not something for nothing, George, I took you in on this, you have to go. That's your thing. I've made the deal with Graff. I can't go. I can't go in, I've spoken on this too much. I've got a big mouth. (*pause*) "The fucking leads" et cetera, "blah blah blah" . . . "the fucking tight ass company . . ."

AARONOW. They'll know when you go over to Graff . . .

Moss. What will they know? That I stole the leads? I *didn't* steal the leads, I'm going to the *movies* tonight with a friend, and then I'm going to the Como Inn. Why did I go to Graff? I got a better deal. *Period.* Let 'em prove something. They can't prove anything that's not the case. (*pause*)

AARONOW. *Dave.*

MOSS. Yes.

AARONOW. You want me to break into the office tonight and steal the leads?

MOSS. Yes. (*pause*)

AARONOW. No.

MOSS. Oh, yes, George.

AARONOW. What does that mean?

MOSS. Listen to this. I have an alibi, I'm going to the Como Inn. Why? The place gets robbed, they're going to come looking for *me.* Why? Because I probably did it. Are you going to turn me in? (*pause*) George? Are you going to turn me in?

AARONOW. What if you don't get caught?

MOSS. They come to you, you going to turn me in?

AARONOW. Why would they come to me?

MOSS. They're going to come to *everyone.*

AARONOW. Why would I *do* it?

MOSS. You wouldn't, George, that's why I'm talking to you. Answer me. They come to you. You going to turn me in?

AARONOW. No.

MOSS. Are you sure?

AARONOW. Yes. I'm sure.

MOSS. Then listen to this: I have to get those leads tonight. That's something I have to do. If I'm not at the *movies* . . . if I'm not eating over at the inn . . . If you don't do this, then *I* have to come in here . . .

AARONOW. . . . you don't have to come in . . .

MOSS. . . . and *rob* the place . . .

AARONOW. . . . I thought that we were only talking . . .

Moss. . . . they *take* me, then. They're going to ask me who were my accomplices.

Aaronow. *Me*?

Moss. Absolutely.

Aaronow. That's ridiculous.

Moss. Well, to the law, you're an accessory. Before the fact.

Aaronow. I didn't ask to be.

Moss. Then tough luck, George, because you are.

Aaronow. Why? *Why*, becuase you only *told* me about it?

Moss. That's right.

Aaronow. Why are you doing this to me, Dave. Why are you talking this way to me? I don't understand. Why are you doing this at *all* . . . ?

Moss. That's none of your fucking business . . .

Aaronow. Well, well, well, *talk* to me, we sat down to eat *dinner*, and here I'm a *criminal* . . .

Moss. You *went* for it.

Aaronow. In the abstract . . .

Moss. So I'm making it concrete.

Aaronow. Why?

Moss. Why? *You* going to give me five grand?

Aaronow. Do you need five grand?

Moss. Is that what I just said?

Aaronow. You need money? Is that the . . .

Moss. Hey, hey, let's just keep it simple, what I need is not the . . . what do *you* need . . . ?

Aaronow. What is the five grand? (*pause*) What is the, you said that we were going to *split* five . . .

Moss. I lied. (*pause*) Alright? My end is *my* business. Your end's twenty-five. In or out. You tell me, you're out you take the consequences.

Aaronow. I do?

Moss. Yes. (*pause*)
AARONOW. And why is that?
Moss. Because you listened.

SCENE 3

*The restaurant. ROMA is seated alone at the booth.
LINGK is at the booth next to him. ROMA is talking to him.*

ROMA. . . . all train compartments smell vaguely of
shit. It gets so you don't mind it. That's the worst thing
that I can confess. You know how long it took me to get
there? A long time. When you *die* you're going to regret
the things you don't do. You think you're *queer* . . . ?
I'm going to tell you something: we're *all* queer. You
think that you're a *thief*? So *what*? You get befuddled
by a middle-class morality . . . ? Get *shut* of it. Shut it
out. You cheated on your wife . . . ? You *did* it, *live* with
it. (*pause*) You fuck little girls, so *be* it. There's an ab-
solute morality? May *be*. And *then* what? If you *think*
there is, then *be* that thing. Bad people go to hell? I
don't *think* so. If you think that, act that way. A hell ex-
ists on earth? Yes. I won't live in it. That's *me*. You ever
take a dump made you feel you'd just slept for twelve
hours . . . ?
LINGK. Did I . . . ?
ROMA. Yes.
LINGK. I don't know.
ROMA. Or a *piss* . . . ? A great meal fades in reflec-
tion. Everything else gains. You know why? 'Cause it's
only food. This shit we eat, it keeps us going. But it's
only food. The great fucks that you may have had.
What do you remember about them?

LINGK. What do I . . . ?

ROMA. Yes.

LINGK. Mmmm . . .

ROMA. I don't know. For *me*, I'm saying, what it is, it's probably not the orgasm. Some broads, forearms on your neck, something her *eyes* did. There was a *sound* she made . . . or, me, lying, in the, I'll tell you: me lying in bed; the next day she brought me café au lait. She gives me a cigarette, my balls feel like concrete. Eh? What I'm saying, what is our life? (*pause*) It's looking foward or it's looking back. And that's our life. That's *it*. Where is the *moment*? (*pause*) And what is it that we're afraid of? Loss. What else? (*pause*) The *bank* closes. We get *sick*, my wife died on a plane, the stock market collapsed. . . . the house burnt down . . . what of these happen . . . ? None of 'em. We worry anyway. What does this mean? I'm not *secure*. How can I be secure? (*pause*) Through amassing wealth beyond all measure? No. And what's beyond all measure? That's a sickness. That's a trap. There is no measure. Only greed. How can we act? The right way, we would say, to deal with this: "There is a one-in-a-million chance that so and so will happen. . . . *Fuck* it, it won't happen to *me*. . . ." No. We know that's not the right way I think. (*pause*) We say the *correct* way to deal with this is "There is a one-in-so-and-so chance this will happen . . . God *protect* me. I am powerless, let it not happen to me. . . ." But no to *that*. I say. There's something else. What is it? "If it happens, AS IT MAY for that is not within our powers, I will *deal* with it, just as I do *today* with what draws my concern today." I say *this* is how we must act. I do those things which seem correct to me *today*. I trust myself. And if security concerns me, I do that which *to-*

day I think will make me secure. And every day I *do* that, when that day *arrives* that I need a reserve, (a) odds are that I have it, and (b) the *true* reserve that I have is the strength that I have of *acting each day* without fear. (*pause*) According to the dictates of my mind. (*pause*) Stocks, bonds, objects of art, real estate. Now: what are they? (*pause*) An opportunity. To what? To make money? Perhaps. To *lose* money? Perhaps. To "indulge" and to "learn" about ourselves? Perhaps. So *fucking what*? What *isn't*? They're an *opportunity*. That's all. They're an *event*. A guy comes up to you, you make a call, you send in a brochure, it doesn't matter, "There're these *properties* I'd like for you to see." What does it mean? What you *want* it to mean. (*pause*) Money? (*pause*) If that's what it signifies to you. Security? (*pause*) Comfort? (*pause*) All it is is THINGS THAT HAPPEN TO YOU. (*pause*) That's all it is. How are they different? (*pause*) Some poor newly married guy gets run down by a cab. Some *busboy* wins the lottery. (*pause*) All it is, it's a carnival. What's special . . . what *draws* us? (*pause*) We're all different. (*pause*) We're not the same. (*pause*) We are not the same. (*pause*) Hmmm. (*pause, sighs*) It's been a long day. (*pause*) What are you drinking?

LINGK. Gimlet.

ROMA. Well, let's have a couple more. My name is Richard Roma, what's yours?

LINGK. Lingk. James Lingk.

ROMA. James. I'm glad to meet you. (*They shake hands.*) I'm glad to meet you. James. (*pause*) I want to show you something. (*pause*) It might mean *nothing* to you . . . and it might not. I don't know. I don't know anymore. (*Pause. He takes out a small map and spreads it on the table.*) What is that? Florida. Glengarry Highlands. Florida. "Florida. *Bullshit.*" And maybe that's true; and that's what *I* said: but look *here*: what is this? This is a piece of land. Listen to what I'm going to tell you now:

ACT TWO

The real estate office. Ransacked. A broken plateglass window boarded up, glass all over the floor. AARONOW and WILLIAMSON standing around, smoking. Pause.

AARONOW. People used to say that there are numbers of such magnitude that multiplying them by two made no difference. (*pause*)

WILLIAMSON. Who used to say that?

AARONOW. In school. (*pause*)

(*BAYLEN, a detective, comes out of the inner office.*)

BAYLEN. Alright . . . ?

(*ROMA enters from the street.*)

ROMA. *Williamson . . . Williamson*, they stole the *contracts* . . . ?

BAYLEN. Excuse me, sir . . .

ROMA. Did they get my contrats?

WILLIAMSON. They got . . .

BAYLEN. Excuse me, fella.

ROMA. . . . did they . . .

BAYLEN. Would you excuse us, please . . . ?

ROMA. Don't *fuck* with me, fella. I'm talking about a fuckin' Cadillac car that you owe me . . .

WILLIAMSON. They didn't get your contract. I filed it before I left.

ROMA. They didn't get my contracts?

WILLIAMSON. They — excuse me . . . (*He goes back into inner room with the detective.*)

ROMA. Oh, *fuck. Fuck.* (*He starts kicking the desk.*) FUCK FUCK FUCK! WILLIAMSON!!! WILLIAM-

SON!!! (*Goes to the door WILLIAMSON went into, tries the door; it's locked.*) OPEN THE FUCKING . . . WILLIAMSON . . .

BAYLEN. (*coming out*) Who are you? (*WILLIAMSON comes out.*)

WILLIAMSON. They didn't get the contracts.

ROMA. Did they . . .

WILLIAMSON. They got, listen to me . . .

ROMA. Th . . .

WILLIAMSON. Listen to me: They got *some* of them.

ROMA. Some of them . . .

BAYLEN. Who told you . . . ?

ROMA. Who told me wh . . . ? You've got a fuckin', you've . . . a . . . who is this . . . ? You've got a board-up on the window. . . . *Moss* told me.

BAYLEN. (*looking back toward the inner office*) *Moss* . . . Who told him?

ROMA. How the fuck do *I* know? (*to WILLIAMSON*) *What . . . talk* to me.

WILLIAMSON. They took *some* of the con . . .

ROMA. . . . some of the contracts . . . Lingk. James Lingk. I closed . . .

WILLIAMSON. You closed him yesterday.

ROMA. Yes.

WILLIAMSON. It went down. I filed it.

ROMA. You did?

WILLIAMSON. Yes.

ROMA. Then I'm over the fucking top and you owe me a Cadillac.

WILLIAMSON. I . . .

ROMA. And I don't want any fucking shit and I don't give a shit, Lingk puts me over the top, you filed it, that's fine, any other shit kicks out *you* go back. You

... *you* reclose it, 'cause I *closed* it and you ... you owe me the car.

BAYLEN. Would you excuse us, please.

AARONOW. I, um, and may ... maybe they're in ... they're in ... you should, John, if we're ins ...

WILLIAMSON. I'm sure that we're insured, George ... (*going back inside*)

ROMA. Fuck insured. You owe me a car.

BAYLEN. (*stepping back into the inner room*) Please don't leave. I'm going to talk to you. What's your name?

ROMA. Are you talking to me? (*pause*)

BAYLEN. Yes. (*pause*)

ROMA. My name is Richard Roma. (*BAYLEN goes back into the inner room.*)

AARONOW. I, you know, they should be insured.

ROMA. What do *you* care ... ?

AARONOW. Then, you know, they wouldn't be so ups ...

ROMA. Yeah. That's swell. Yes. You're right. (*pause*) How are you?

AARONOW. I'm fine. You mean the *board*? You mean the *board* ... ?

ROMA. I don't ... yes. Okay, the board.

AARONOW. I'm, I'm, I'm, I'm fucked on the board. *You.* You see how ... I ... (*pause*) I can't ... my mind must be in other places. 'Cause I can't do any ...

ROMA. *What*? You can't do any *what*? (*pause*)

AARONOW. I can't close 'em.

ROMA. Well, they're old. I saw the shit that they were giving you.

AARONOW. Yes.

ROMA. Huh?

AARONOW. Yes. They are old.

ROMA. They're ancient.

AARONOW. Clear . . .

ROMA. Clear Meadows. That shit's dead. (*pause*)

AARONOW. It *is* dead.

ROMA. It's a waste of time.

AARONOW. Yes. (*long pause*) I'm no fucking good.

ROMA. That's . . .

AARONOW. Everything I . . . *you* know . . .

ROMA. That's not . . . Fuck that shit, George. You're a, *hey*, you had a bad month. You're a good man, George.

AARONOW. I am?

ROMA. You hit a bad streak. We've all . . . look at this: fifteen units Mountain View, the fucking things get stole.

AARONOW. He said he filed . . .

ROMA. He filed half of them, he file the *big* one. All the little ones, I have, I have to go back and . . . ah, *fuck*, I got to go out like a fucking schmuck hat in my hand and reclose the . . . (*pause*) I mean, talk about a bad streak. That would sap *anyone's* self confi . . . I got to go out and reclose all my . . . Where's the phones?

AARONOW. They stole . . .

ROMA. They stole the . . .

AARONOW. What. What kind of outfit are we running where . . . where anyone . . .

ROMA. (*to himself*) They stole the phones.

AARONOW. Where criminals can come in here . . . they take the . . .

ROMA. They stole the phones. They stole the leads. They're . . . *Christ.* (*pause*) What am I going to do this month? Oh, *shit* . . . (*starts for the door*)

AARONOW. You think they're going to catch . . . where are you going?

ROMA. Down the street.

WILLIAMSON. (*sticking his head out of the door*) Where are you going?

ROMA. To the restaura . . . what do you fucking . . . ?

WILLIAMSON. Aren't you going out today?

ROMA. With what? (*pause*) With what, John, they took the leads . . .

WILLIAMSON. I have the stuff from last year's . . .

ROMA. Oh. Oh. Oh, your "nostalgia" file, that's fine. No. Swell. 'Cause I don't have to . . .

WILLIAMSON. . . . you want to go out today . . . ?

ROMA. 'Cause I don't have to *eat* this month. No. Okay. *Give* 'em to me . . . (*to himself*) Fucking Mitch and Murray going to shit a br . . . what am I going to *do* all . . . (*WILLIAMSON starts back into the office. He is accosted by AARONOW.*)

AARONOW. Were the leads . . .

ROMA. . . . what am I going to *do* all month . . . ?

AARONOW. Were the leads insured?

WILLIAMSON. I don't know, George, why?

AARONOW. 'Cause, you know, 'cause they weren't, I know that Mitch and Murray uh . . . (*pause*)

WILLIAMSON. What?

AARONOW. That they're going to be upset.

WILLIAMSON. That's right. (*Going back into his office, pause; to ROMA:*) You want to go out today . . . ? (*Pause, WILLIAMSON returns to his office.*)

AARONOW. He said we're all going to have to go talk to the guy.

ROMA. What?

AARONOW. He said we . . .

ROMA. To the cop?

AARONOW. Yeah.

ROMA. Yeah. That's swell. *Another* waste of time.

AARONOW. A waste of time? Why?

ROMA. *Why*? 'Cause they aren't going to find the guy.

AARONOW. The cops?

ROMA. Yes. The cops. No.

AARONOW. They aren't?

ROMA. No.

AARONOW. Why don't you think so?

ROMA. Why? Because they're *stupid*. "Where were you last night . . ."

AARONOW. Where were you?

ROMA. Where was *I*?

AARONOW. Yes.

ROMA. I was at home, where were *you*?

AARONOW. At home.

ROMA. *See* . . . ? Were you the guy who broke in?

AARONOW. Was I?

ROMA. Yes.

AARONOW. No.

ROMA. Then don't sweat it, George, you know why?

AARONOW. No.

ROMA. You have nothing to hide.

AARONOW. (*pause*) When I talk to the police, I get nervous.

ROMA. Yeah. You know who doesn't?

AARONOW. No, who?

ROMA. Thieves.

AARONOW. Why?

ROMA. They're inured to it.

AARONOW. You think so?

ROMA. Yes. (*pause*)

AARONOW. But what should I *tell* them?

ROMA. The truth, George. Always tell the truth. It's the easiest thing to remember. (*WILLIAMSON comes out of the office with leads. ROMA takes one, reads it.*)

ROMA. *Patel*? Ravidam *Patel*? How am I going to

make a living on these deadbeat *wogs*? Where did you get this, from the *morgue*?

WILLIAMSON. If you don't want it, give it back.

ROMA. I don't "want" it, if you catch my drift.

WILLIAMSON. I'm giving you *three* leads. You . . .

ROMA. What's the fucking point in *any* case . . . ? What's the *point*. I got to argue with *you*, I got to knock heads with the *cops*, I'm busting my *balls*, sell your *dirt* to fucking *deadbeats* money in the *mattress*, I come back you can't even manage to keep the contracts safe, I have to go back and close them *again*. . . . What the fuck am I wasting my time, fuck this shit. I'm going out and reclose last week's . . .

WILLIAMSON. The word from Murray is: leave them alone. If we need a new signature he'll go out himself, he'll be the *president*, just come *in*, from out of *town* . . .

ROMA. Okay, okay, okay, gimme this shit. Fine. (*takes the leads*)

WILLIAMSON. Now, I'm giving you three . . .

ROMA. Three? I count *two*.

WILLIAMSON. Three.

ROMA. Patel? Fuck *you*. Fuckin' *Shiva* handed him a million dollars, told him "sign the deal," he wouldn't sign. And Vishnu, too. Into the bargain. Fuck *that*, John. You know your business, I know mine. Your business is being an *asshole*, and I find out whose fucking *cousin* you are, I'm going to go to him and figure out a way to have your *ass* . . . fuck you—I'll wait for the new leads.

(*SHELLY LEVENE enters.*)

LEVENE. Get the *chalk*. Get the *chalk* . . . get the chalk! I closed 'em! I *closed* the cocksucker. Get the

chalk and put me on the *board*. I'm going to Hawaii!
Put me on the Cadillac board, Williamson! Pick up the
fuckin' chalk. Eight units. Mountain View . . .

ROMA. You sold eight Mountain View?

LEVENE. You bet your ass. Who wants to go to lunch?
Who wants to go to lunch? I'm buying. (*slaps contract
down on WILLIAMSON's desk*) Eighty-two fucking
grand. And twelve grand in commission. John. (*pause*)
On fucking deadbeat magazine subscription leads.

WILLIAMSON. Who?

LEVENE. (*pointing to contract*) *Read* it. Bruce and
Harriett Nyborg. (*looking around*) What happened
here?

AARONOW. Fuck. I had them on River Glen. (*LE-
VENE looks around*)

LEVENE. What happened?

WILLIAMSON. Somebody broke in.

ROMA. Eight units?

LEVENE. That's right.

ROMA. *Shelly* . . . !

LEVENE. Hey, big fucking deal. Broke a bad streak
. . .

AARONOW. Shelly, the Machine, Levene.

LEVENE. You . . .

AARONOW. That's great.

LEVENE. Thank you, George.

(*BAYLEN sticks his head out of the room; calls in,
"Aaronow."*)

LEVENE. Williamson, get on the phone, call Mitch . . .

ROMA. They took the phones . . .

LEVENE. They . . .

BAYLEN. *Aaronow* . . .

ROMA. They took the typewriters, they took the leads, they took the *cash*, they took the *contracts* . . .

LEVENE. Wh . . . wh . . . Wha . . . ?

AARONOW. We had a robbery. (*goes into the inner room*)

LEVENE. (*pause*) When?

ROMA. Last night, this morning. (*pause*)

LEVENE. They took the leads?

ROMA. Mmm.

(*MOSS comes out of the interrogation.*)

MOSS. Fuckin' asshole.

ROMA. What, they beat you with a rubber bat?

MOSS. Cop couldn't find his dick two hands and a map. Anyone talks to this guy's an *asshole* . . .

ROMA. You going to turn State's?

MOSS. Fuck you, Ricky. I ain't going out today. I'm going home. I'm going home because nothing'g *accomplished* here. . . . Anyone *talks* to this guy is . . .

ROMA. Guess what the Machine did?

MOSS. Fuck the Machine.

ROMA. Mountain View. Eight units.

MOSS. Fuckin' cop's got no right talk to me that way. I didn't rob the place . . .

ROMA. You hear what I said?

MOSS. Yeah. He closed a deal.

ROMA. Eight units. Mountain View.

MOSS. (*to LEVENE*) You did that?

LEVENE. Yeah. (*pause*)

MOSS. Fuck you.

ROMA. Guess who?

MOSS. When . . . ?

LEVENE. Just now.

ROMA. Guess who?

Moss. You just this morning . . .

ROMA. Harriet and blah blah Nyborg.

Moss. You did that?

LEVENE. Eighty-two thousand dollars. (*pause*)

Moss. Those fuckin' *deadbeats* . . .

LEVENE. My ass, I told 'em. (*to ROMA*) Listen to this: I said . . .

Moss. Hey, I don't want to hear your fucking war stories . . .

ROMA. Fuck *you*, Dave . . .

LEVENE. "You have to believe in your*self* . . . you" — look — "alright . . . ?"

Moss. (*to WILLIAMSON*) Give me some leads. I'm going out . . . I'm getting out of . . .

LEVENE. ". . . you have to believe in your*self* . . ."

Moss. Na, fuck the leads, I'm going home.

LEVENE. "Bruce, Harriet . . . Fuck *me*, believe in your*self* . . ."

ROMA. We haven't got a lead . . .

Moss. Why not?

ROMA. They took 'em . . .

Moss. Hey, they're fuckin' garbage any case. . . . This whole goddamn . . .

LEVENE. ". . . You look around, you say, 'This one has so-and-so, and I have nothing . . . '"

Moss. *Shit.*

LEVENE. "'*Why*? Why don't I get the opportunities . . . ?'"

Moss. And did they steal the contracts . . . ?

ROMA. Fuck *you* care . . . ?

LEVENE. "I want to tell you something, Harriett . . ."

Moss. . . . the fuck is *that* supposed to mean . . . ?

LEVENE. Will you shut up, I'm telling you this . . .

(*AARONOW sticks his head out.*)

AARONOW. Can we get some coffee . . . ?

Moss. How ya doing? (*pause*)

AARONOW. Fine.

Moss. Uh-huh.

AARONOW. If anyone's going, I could use some coffee.

LEVENE. "You *do* get the . . ." (*to ROMA*) Huh? Huh?

Moss. *Fuck* is that supposed to mean?

LEVENE. "You *do* get the opportunity. . . . You *get* them. As *I* do, as *anyone* does . . ."

Moss. Ricky? . . . That I don't care they stole the contracts? (*pause*)

LEVENE. I got 'em in the kitchen. I'm eating her crumb cake.

Moss. What does that mean?

ROMA. It *means*, Dave, you haven't closed a good one in a month, none of my business, you want to push me to answer you. (*pause*) And so you haven't got a contract to get stolen or so forth.

Moss. You have a mean streak in you, Ricky, you know that . . . ?

LEVENE. Rick. Let me tell you. Wait, we're in the . . .

Moss. Shut the fuck up. (*pause*) Ricky. You have a mean streak in you. . . . (*to LEVENE*) And what the fuck are *you* babbling about . . . ? (*to ROMA*) Bring that shit up. Of my volume. You were on a bad one and I brought it up to *you* you'd harbor it. (*pause*) You'd harbor it a long long while. And you'd be right.

ROMA. Who said "Fuck the Machine"?

Moss. "*Fuck the Machine*"? "*Fuck the Machine*"? What is this. *Courtesy* class . . . ? You're *fucked*, Rick — are you fucking *nuts*? You're hot, so you think you're the *ruler* of this place . . . ?! You want to . . .

LEVENE. Dave . . .

Moss. . . . Shut up. Decide who should be dealt with how? Is that the thing? I come into the fuckin' office today, I get humiliated by some jagoff cop. I get accused of . . . I get this *shit* thrown in my face by you, you genuine shit, because you're top name on the board . . .

ROMA. Is that what I did? Dave? I humiliated you? My *God* . . . I'm *sorry* . . .

Moss. Sittin' on top of the *world*, sittin' on top of the *world*, everything's fucking *peach*fuzz . . .

ROMA. Oh, and I don't get a moment to spare for a bust-out *humanitarian* down on his luck lately. Fuck *you*, Dave, you know you got a big *mouth*. And *you* make a close the whole *place* stinks with your *farts* for a week. "How much you just ingested," what a big *man* you are, "Hey, let me buy you a pack of gum. I'll show you how to *chew* it." Your *pal* closes, all that comes out of your mouth is *bile*, how fucked *up* you are . . .

Moss. *Who's* my pal . . . ? And what are you, Ricky, huh, what are you, Bishop *Sheean*? Who the fuck are *you*, Mr. Slick . . . ? What are you, friend to the *workingman*? Big deal. Fuck *you*, you got the memory a fuckin' *fly*. I never liked you.

ROMA. What is this, your farewell speech?

Moss. I'm going home.

ROMA. Your farewell to the troops?

Moss. I'm not going home. I'm going to Wis*con*sin.

ROMA. Have a good trip.

Moss. (*simultaneously with "trip"*) And fuck *you*. Fuck the *lot* of you. Fuck you *all*. (*MOSS exits. Pause.*)

ROMA. (*to LEVENE*) You were saying? (*pause*) Come on. Come on, you got them in the kitchen, you got the stats spread out, you're in your shirtsleeves, you can *smell* it. Huh? Snap out of it, you're eating her *crumb* cake. (*pause*)

LEVENE. I'm eating her *crumb* cake . . .

ROMA. How was it . . . ?

LEVENE. From the store.

ROMA. Fuck *her* . . .

LEVENE. "What we have to do is *admit* to ourself that we see that opportunity . . . and *take* it. (*pause*) And that's it." And we *sit* there. (*pause*) I got the pen out . . .

ROMA. "Always be closing . . ."

LEVENE. That's what I'm *saying*. The *old* ways. The *old* ways . . . convert the motherfucker . . . *sell* him . . . *sell* him . . . *make him sign the check*. (*pause*) The . . . Bruce, Harriett . . . the kitchen, blah: they got their money in *government* bonds. . . . I say *fuck* it, we're going to go the whole route. I plat it out eight units. Eighty-two grand. I tell them. "This is now. This is that *thing* that you've been dreaming of, you're going to find that suitcase on the train, the guy comes in the door, the bag that's full of money. This is it, *Harriett* . . ."

ROMA. (*reflectively*) Harriett . . .

LEVENE. *Bruce* . . . "I don't want to fuck *around* with you. I don't want to go *round* this, and pussyfoot *around* the thing, you have to look back on this. I do, too. I came here to do good for you and me. For *both* of us. Why take an interim position? *The only arrangement I'll accept* is full investment. Period. The whole eight units. I know that you're saying 'be safe,' I know what you're saying. I know if I left you to yourselves, you'd say 'come back tomorrow,' and when I walked out that door, you'd make a cup of *coffee* . . . you'd sit *down* . . . and you'd think 'let's be safe . . .' and not to disappoint me you'd go *one* unit or maybe two, because you'd become scared because you'd met possi*bil*ity. But this won't do, and that's not the subject. . . ." Listen to this, I actually said this. "That's not the subject of our *evening* together." Now I handed them the pen. I held it in my hand. I turned the contract, eight units eighty-two grand. "Now I want you to sign." (*pause*) I sat there. Five minutes. Then, I sat there, Ricky, *twenty-two minutes* by the kitchen *clock*. (*pause*) Twenty-two minutes by the kitchen clock. Not a *word*, not a *motion*. What am I thinking? "My arm's getting tired?" *No*. I *did* it. I *did* it. Like in the *old* days, Ricky. Like I was taught . . . Like, like, like, I *used* to do . . . I did it.

ROMA. Like you taught me . . .

LEVENE. Bullshit, you're . . . No. That's . . . that's . . . well, if I *did*, then I'm *glad* I did. I, *well*. I locked on them. All on them, nothing no me. All my thoughts are on them. I'm holding the last thought that I spoke: "Now is the time." (*pause*) They signed, Ricky. It was *great*. It was fucking great. It was like they wilted all at once. No *gesture* . . . nothing. Like together. They, I swear to God, they both kind of *imperceptibly slumped*. And he reaches and takes the pen and signs, he passes it to her, she signs. It was so fucking solemn. I just let it sit. I nod like this. I nod again. I grasp his hands. I shake his hands. I grasp *her* hands. I nod at her like this. "Bruce . . . Harriett . . ." I'm beaming at them. I'm nodding like this. I point back in the living room, back to the sideboard. (*pause*) *I didn't fucking know there was a sideboard there*!! He goes back, he brings us a drink. Little shot glasses. A pattern in 'em. And we toast. In silence. (*pause*)

ROMA. That was a great sale, Shelly. (*pause*)

LEVENE. Ah, fuck. Leads! Leads! Williamson! (*WILLIAMSON sticks his head out of the office.*) Send me *out*! Send me *out*!

WILLIAMSON. The leads are coming.

LEVENE. *Get* 'em to me!

WILLIAMSON. I talked to Murray and Mitch an hour ago. They're coming in, you understand they're a bit *upset* over this morning's . . .

LEVENE. Did you tell 'em my sale?

WILLIAMSON. How could I tell 'em your sale? Eh? I don't have a tel . . . I'll tell 'em your sale when they bring in the leads. Alright? Shelly. Alright? We had a little . . . You closed a deal. You made a good sale. Fine.

LEVENE. It's better than a good sale. It's a . . .

WILLIAMSON. Look: I have a lot of things on my mind, they're coming in, alright, they're very upset, I'm trying to make some *sense* . . .

LEVENE. All that I'm *telling* you: that one thing you can tell them it's a remarkable sale.

WILLIAMSON. The only thing remarkable is who you made it to.

LEVENE. What does *that* fucking mean?

WILLIAMSON. That if the sale sticks, it will be a miracle.

LEVENE. Why should the sale not stick? Hey, *fuck* you. That's what I'm saying. You have no idea of your job. A man's his job and you're *fucked* at yours. You hear what I'm saying to you? Your "end of the month board . . ." You can't run an office. I don't care. You don't know what it *is*, you don't have the *sense*, you don't have the *balls*. You ever been on a sit? *Ever*? Has this cocksucker ever been . . . you ever sit down with a cust . . .

WILLIAMSON. I were you, I'd calm down, Shelly.

LEVENE. *Would* you? *Would* you . . . ? Or you're gonna *what*, fire me?

WILLIAMSON. It's not impossible.

LEVENE. On an eighty-thousand dollar *day*? And it ain't even *noon*.

ROMA. You closed 'em today?

LEVENE. Yes. I did. This *morning*. (*to WILLIAM-SON*) What I'm *saying* to you: things can *change*. You *see*? This is where you fuck *up*, because this is something you don't *know*. You can't look down the *road*. And see what's *coming*. Might be someone *else*, John. It might be someone *new*, eh? Someone *new*. And you can't look *back*. 'Cause you don't know *history*. You ask them. When we were at Rio Rancho, who was top man? A month . . . ? Two months . . . ? Eight months in twelve for three years in a row. You know what that means? You know what that means? Is that *luck*? Is that some, some, some purloined leads? That's *skill*. That's *talent*, that's, that's . . .

ROMA. . . . *yes* . . .

LEVENE. . . . and you don't *remember*. 'Cause you weren't *around*. That's cold *calling*. Walk up to the door. I don't even know their *name*. I'm selling something they don't even *want*. You talk about soft sell . . . before we had a name for it . . . before we called it anything, we did it.

ROMA. That's right, Shel.

LEVENE. And, and, and, I *did* it. And I put a kid through *school*. My *daughter* . . . She . . . and . . . Cold *calling*, fella. Door to door. But you don't know. You don't know. You never heard of a *streak*. You never heard of "marshaling your sales force. . . ." What are you, you're a *secretary*, John. Fuck *you*. That's my message to you. Fuck you and kiss my ass. You don't like it, I'll go talk to Jerry Graff. Period. Fuck you. Put me on the board. And I want three worthwhile leads today and I don't want any bullshit about them and I want 'em close together 'cause I'm going to hit them all today. That's all I have to say to you.

ROMA. He's right, Williamson. (*WILLIAMSON goes into a side office. Pause.*)

LEVENE. It's not right. I'm sorry, and I'll tell you who's to blame is Mitch and Murray. (*ROMA sees something outside the window.*)

ROMA. (*sotto*) Oh, Christ.

LEVENE. The hell with him. We'll go to lunch, the leads won't be up for . . .

ROMA. You're a client. I just sold you five waterfront Glengarry Farms. I rub my head, throw me the cue "Kenilworth."

LEVENE. What is it?

ROMA. Kenilw . . . (*LINGK enters the office.*)

ROMA. (*to LEVENE*) *I* own the property, my *mother* owns the property, I put her *into* it. I'm going to show you on the plats. You look when you get home A-3 through A-14 and 26 through 30. You take your time and if you still feel.

LEVENE. No, Mr. Roma. I don't need the time, I've made a lot of *investments* in the last . . .

LINGK. I've got to talk to you.

ROMA. (*looking up*) Jim! What are you doing here? Jim Lingk, D. Ray Morton . . .

LEVENE. Glad to meet you.

ROMA. I just put Jim into Black Creek . . . are you acquainted with . . .

LEVENE. No . . . Black *Creek*. Yes. In *Florida*?

ROMA. Yes.

LEVENE. I wanted to *speak* with you about . . .

ROMA. Well, we'll do that this weekend.

LEVENE. My *wife* told me to look into . . .

ROMA. *Beautiful.* Beautiful rolling land. I was telling Jim and Jinny, Ray, I want to tell you something. (*to LEVENE*) You, Ray, you eat in a lot of restaurants. I

know you do. ... (*to LINGK*) Mr. Morton's with
American Express ... he's ... (*to LEVENE*) I can tell
Jim what you do ... ?

LEVENE. Sure.

ROMA. Ray is director of all European sales and ser-
vices for American Ex ... (*to LEVENE*) But I'm saying
you haven't had a *meal* until you've tasted ... I was at
the Lingk's last ... as a matter of fact, what was that
service feature you were talking about ... ?

LEVENE. Which ...

ROMA. "Home Cooking" ... what did you call it, you
said ... it was a tag phrase that you had ...

LEVENE. Uh ...

ROMA. Home ...

LEVENE. Home cooking ...

ROMA. The monthly interview ... ?

LEVENE. Oh! For the *magazine* ...

ROMA. Yes. Is this something that I can talk ab ...

LEVENE. Well, it isn't coming *out* until the February
iss ... *sure*. Sure, go ahead, Rick.

ROMA. You're sure?

LEVENE. (*nods*) Go ahead.

ROMA. Well, Ray was eating at one of his company's
men's home in France ... the man's French, isn't he?

LEVENE. No, his *wife* is.

ROMA. Ah. Ah, his wife is. Ray: what *time* do you
have ... ?

LEVENE. Twelve-fifteen.

ROMA. Oh! My God ... I've got to get you on the
plane!

LEVENE. Didn't I say I was taking the two o' ...

ROMA. No. You said the one. That's why you said we
couldn't talk till Kenilworth.

LEVENE. Oh, my God, you're right! I'm on the one.
... (*getting up*) Well, let's *scoot* ...

LINGK. I've got to talk to you . . .

ROMA. I've got to get Ray to O'Hare . . . (*to LE-VENE*) Come on, let's hustle. . . . (*over his shoulder*) John! Call American Express in *Pittsburgh* for Mr. Morton, will you, tell them he's on the one o'clock. (*to LINGK*) I'll see you. . . . Christ, I'm sorry you came all the way in. . . . I'm running Ray over to O'Hare. . . . You wait here, I'll . . . no. (*to LEVENE*) I'm meeting your man at the back. . . . (*to LINGK*) I wish you'd phoned. . . . I'll tell you, wait: are you and Jinny going to be home tonight? (*rubs forehead*)

LINGK. I . . .

LEVENE. Rick.

ROMA. What?

LEVENE. *Kenilworth* . . . ?

ROMA. I'm sorry . . . ?

LEVENE. *Kenilworth.*

ROMA. Oh, God . . . Oh, God . . . (*ROMA takes LINGK aside, sotto*) Jim, excuse me. . . . Ray, I told you, who he is is *the* senior vice-president American Express. His family owns 32 per. . . . Over the past years I've sold him . . . I can't tell you the dollar amount, but *quite* a lot of land. I promised five *weeks* ago that I'd go to the wife's birthday party in Kenilworth tonight. (*sighs*) I *have* to go. You understand. They treat me like a member of the family, so I have to go. It's funny, you know, you get a picture of the Corporation-Type Company Man, all business . . . this man, *no.* We'll go out to his home sometime. Let's see. (*He checks his datebook.*) Tomorrow. No. Tomorrow, I'm in L.A. . . . *Monday* . . . I'll take you to lunch, where would you like to go?

LINGK. My wife . . . (*ROMA rubs his head.*)

LEVENE. (*standing in the door*) Rick . . . ?

ROMA. I'm sorry, Jim. I can't talk now. I'll call you tonight . . . I'm sorry. I'm coming, Ray. (*starts for the door*)

LINGK. My wife said I have to cancel the deal.

ROMA. It's a common reaction, Jim. I'll tell you what it is, and I know that that's why you married her. One of the reasons is *prudence*. It's a sizable investment. One *thinks* twice . . . it's also something *women* have. It's just a reaction to the size of the investment. *Monday,* if you'd invite me for dinner again . . . (*to LEVENE*) This woman can *cook* . . .

LEVENE. (*simultaneously*) I'm sure she can . . .

ROMA. (*to LINGK*) We're going to talk. I'm going to *tell* you something. Because (*sotto*) there's something about your acreage I want you to know. I can't talk about it now. I really shouldn't. And, in fact, by *law*, I . . . (*shrugs, resigned*) The man next to you, he bought his lot at forty-*two*, he phoned to say that he'd *already* had an offer . . . (*ROMA rubs his head.*)

LEVENE. Rick . . . ?

ROMA. I'm coming, Ray . . . what a day! I'll cal you this evening, Jim. I'm sorry you had to come in . . . Monday, lunch.

LINGK. My wife . . .

LEVENE. Rick, we really have to go.

LINGK. My wife . . .

ROMA. Monday.

LINGK. She called the consumer . . . the attorney, I don't know. The attorney gen . . . they said we have three days . . .

ROMA. *Who* did she call?

LINGK. I don't know, the attorney gen . . . the . . . some consumer office.

ROMA. Why did she do *that*, Jim?

LINGK. I don't know (*pause*) They said we have three days. (*pause*) They said we have three days.

ROMA. Three days.

LINGK. To ... you know (*pause*)

ROMA. No, I don't know. *Tell* me.

LINGK. To change our minds.

ROMA. Of *course* you have three days. (*pause*)

LINGK. So we can't talk *Monday. (pause)*

ROMA. Jim, Jim, you saw my book ... I *can't, you* saw my book ...

LINGK. But we have to *before* Monday. To get our money ba ...

ROMA. Three *business* days. They mean three *business* days.

LINGK. Wednesday, Thursday, Friday.

ROMA. I don't understand.

LINGK. That's what they are. Three business ... if I wait till Monday, my time limit runs out.

ROMA. You don't count Saturday.

LINGK. I'm not.

ROMA. No, I'm saying you don't include Saturday ... in your three days. It's not a *business* day.

LINGK. But I'm not *counting* it. (*pause*) Wednesday. Thursday. Friday. So it would have elapsed.

ROMA. What would have elapsed?

LINGK. If we wait till Mon ...

ROMA. When did you write the check?

LINGK. Yest ...

ROMA. What was yesterday?

LINGK. Tuesday.

ROMA. And when was that check cashed?

LINGK. I don't know.

ROMA. What was the *earliest* it could have been cashed? (*pause*)

LINGK. I don't know.

ROMA. *Today.* (*pause*) *Today.* Which, in any case, it was not, as there were a couple of points on the agreement I wanted to go over with you in any case.

LINGK. The check wasn't cashed?

ROMA. I just called downtown, and it's on their desk.

LEVENE. Rick . . .

ROMA. One moment, I'll be right with you. (*to LINGK*) In fact, a . . . *one* point, which I spoke to you of which (*looks around*) I can't talk to you about here.

(*DETECTIVE puts his head out of the doorway.*)

BAYLEN. Levene!!!

LINGK. I, I . . .

ROMA. Listen to me, the *statute*, it's for your protection. I have no complaints with that, in fact, I was a member of the board when we *drafted* it, so quite the *opposite.* It *says* that you can change your mind three working days from the time the deal is closed.

BAYLEN. Levene!

ROMA. Which, wait a second, which is not until the check is cashed.

BAYLEN. Levene!!

(*AARONOW comes out of the DETECTIVE's office.*)

AARONOW. I'm *through*, with *this* fucking meshugaas. No one should talk to a man that way. How are you *talking* to me that . . . ?

BAYLEN. Levene! (*WILLIAMSON puts his head out of the office.*)

AARONOW. . . . how can you *talk* to me that . . . that . . .

LEVENE. (*to ROMA*) Rick, I'm going to flag a cab.

AARONOW. *I* didn't rob . . . (*WILLIAMSON sees LE-VENE.*)

WILLIAMSON. Shelly: get in the office.

AARONOW. *I* didn't . . . why should *I* . . . "Where were you last . . ." Is anybody listening to me . . . ? Where's Moss . . . ? Where . . . ?

BAYLEN. Levene? (*to WILLIAMSON*) Is this Lev . . . (*BAYLEN accosts LINGK.*)

LEVENE. (*taking BAYLEN into the office*) Ah. Ah. Perhaps I can advise you on that. . . . (*to ROMA and LINGK, as he exits*) *Excuse* us, will you . . . ?

AARONOW. (*simultaneous with LEVENE's speech above*) . . . Come in here . . . I *work* here, I don't come in here to be *mistreated* . . .

WILLIAMSON. Go to *lunch*, will you . . .

AARONOW. I want to *work* today, that's why I came . . .

WILLIAMSON. The leads come in, I'll let . . .

AARONOW. . . . that's why I came in. I thought I . . .

WILLIAMSON. Just go to lunch.

AARONOW. I don't *want* to go to lunch.

WILLIAMSON. Go to lunch, George.

AARONOW. Where does he get off to talk that way to a working man? It's not . . .

WILLIAMSON. (*buttonholes him*) Will you take it outside, we have people trying to do *business* here . . .

AARONOW. That's what, that's what, that's what *I* was trying to do. (*pause*) That's why I came *in* . . . I meet *gestapo* tac . . .

WILLIAMSON. (*going back into his office*) Excuse me . . .

AARONOW. I meet *gestapo* tactics . . . I meet *gestapo* tactics. . . . That's not right. . . . No man has the right to

... "Call an attorney," that means you're guilt ... you're under sus ... "Co ..." he says, "cooperate" or we'll go downtown. *That's* not ... as long as I've ...

WILLIAMSON. (*bursting out of his office*) Will you get out of here. Will you get *out* of here. Will you. I'm trying to run an *office* here. Will you go to lunch? Go to lunch. Will you go to lunch? (*retreats into office*)

ROMA. (*to AARONOW*) Will you excuse ...

AARONOW. Where did Moss ... ? I ...

ROMA. Will you excuse me please?

AARONOW. Uh, uh, did he go to the restaurant? (*pause*) I ... I ... (*exits*)

ROMA. I'm *very* sorry, Jimmy. I apologize to you.

LINGK. It's not me, it's my wife.

ROMA. (*pause*) What is?

LINGK. I told you.

ROMA. Tell me again.

LINGK. What's going on here?

ROMA. Tell me again. Your wife.

LINGK. I told you.

ROMA. You tell me again.

LINGK. She wants her money back.

ROMA. We're going to speak to her.

LINGK. No. She told me "right now."

ROMA. We'll speak to her, Jim ...

LINGK. She won't listen.

(*DETECTIVE sticks his head out.*)

BAYLEN. *Roma.*

LINGK. She told me if not, I have to call the State's attorney.

Roma. No, no. That's just something she "said." We don't have to do that.

Lingk. She told me I *have* to.

Roma. No, Jim.

Lingk. I *do*. If I don't get my *money* back . . .

Baylen. Roma! (*to ROMA*) I'm talking to you . . .

Roma. I've . . . look. (*generally*) Will someone get this guy off my back.

Baylen. You have a problem?

Roma. Yes, I have a problem. Yes, I *do*, my fr . . . It's not me that ripped the joint off, I'm doing *business*. I'll be with you in a *while*. You got it . . . ? (*DETECTIVE goes back into inner office. Looks back, LINGK is heading for the door.*) Where are you going?

Lingk. I'm . . .

Roma. Where are you going . . . ? This is *me*. . . . This is Ricky, Jim. Jim, anything you *want*, you *want* it, you *have* it. You understand? This is *me*. Something *upset* you. Sit down, now sit down. You tell me what it is. (*pause*) Am I going to help you fix it? You're goddamned right I am. Sit down. Tell you something . . . ? *Sometimes* we need someone from *outside*. It's . . . no, sit down. . . . Now *talk* to me.

Lingk. I can't negotiate.

Roma. What does that mean?

Lingk. That . . .

Roma. . . . what, what, *say* it. Say it to me . . .

Lingk. I . . .

Roma. What . . . ?

Lingk. I . . .

Roma. What . . . ? Say the words.

Lingk. I don't have the *power*. (*pause*) I said it.

Roma. What power?

LINGK. The power to negotiate.

ROMA. To negotiate what? (*pause*) To negotiate what?

LINGK. *This.*

ROMA. What, "this"? (*pause*)

LINGK. The deal.

ROMA. The "deal," *forget* the deal. *Forget* the deal, you've got something on your mind, Jim, what is it?

LINGK. (*rising*) I can't talk to you, *you* met my wife, I . . . (*pause*)

ROMA. What? (*pause*) What? (*pause*) What, Jim: I tell you what, let's get out of here . . . let's go get a drink.

LINGK. She told me not to talk to you.

ROMA. Let's . . . no one's going to know, let's go around the *corner* and we'll get a drink.

LINGK. She told me I had to get back the check or call the State's att . . .

ROMA. *Forget* the deal, Jimmy. (*pause*) *Forget* the deal . . . you know me. The deal's *dead*. Am I talking about the *deal*? That's *over*. Please. Let's talk about *you*. Come on. (*Pause. ROMA rises and starts walking toward the front door.*) Come on. (*pause*) Come on, Jim. (*pause*) I want to tell you something. You life is your own. You have a contract with your wife. You have certain things you do *jointly*, you have a *bond* there . . . and there are *other* things. Those things are yours. You needn't feel *ashamed*, you needn't feel that you're being *untrue* . . . or that she would abandon you if she knew. This is *your* life. (*pause*) Yes. Now I want to *talk* to you because you're obviously upset and that *concerns* me. Now let's go. Right now. (*LINGK gets up and they start for the door.*)

BAYLEN. (*sticks his head out of the door*) Roma . . .

LINGK. . . . and . . . and . . . (*pause*)

ROMA. What?

LINGK. And the check is . . .

ROMA. What did I *tell* you? (*pause*) What did I say about the three days . . . ?

BAYLEN. Roma, would you, I'd like to get some lunch . . .

ROMA. I'm talking with Mr. Lingk. If you please, I'll be back in. (*checks watch*) I'll be back in a while. . . . I told you, check with Mr. Williamson.

BAYLEN. The people downtown said . . .

ROMA. You call them again. Mr. Williamson . . . !

WILLIAMSON. (*coming out of his office*) Yes.

ROMA. Mr. Lingk and I are going to . . .

WILLIAMSON. Yes. Please. Please. (*to LINGK*) The police (*shrugs*) can be . . .

LINGK. What are the police doing?

ROMA. It's nothing.

LINGK. What are the *police* doing here . . . ?

WILLIAMSON. We had a slight burglary last night.

ROMA. It was nothing . . . I was assuring Mr. Lingk . . .

WILLIAMSON. Mr. Lingk. James Lingk. Your contract went out. Nothing to . . .

ROMA. John . . .

WILLIAMSON. Your contract went out to the bank.

LINGK. You cashed the check?

WILLIAMSON. We . . .

ROMA. . . . Mr. Williamson . . .

WILLIAMSON. Your check was cashed yesterday afternoon. And we're completely insured, as you know, in *any* case. (*pause*)

LINGK. (*to ROMA*) You cashed the check?

ROMA. Not to my knowledge, no . . .

WILLIAMSON. I'm sure we can . . .

LINGK. Oh, Christ . . . (*starts out the door*) Don't follow me. . . . Oh, Christ. (*pause, to ROMA*) I know I've let you down. I'm sorry. For . . . Forgive . . . for . . . I don't know anymore. (*pause*) Forgive me. (*LINGK exits. Pause.*)

ROMA. (*to WILLIAMSON*) You stupid fucking cunt. *You*, Williamson . . . I'm talking to *you*, shithead. . . . You just cost me *six thousand dollars*. (*pause*) Six thousand dollars. And one Cadillac. That's right. What are you going to do about it? What are you going to do about it, asshole. You fucking *shit*. Where did you learn your *trade*? You stupid fucking *cunt*. You *idiot*. Whoever told you you could work with *men*?

BAYLEN. Could I . . .

ROMA. I'm going to have your *job*, shithead. I'm going *downtown* and talk to Mitch and Murray, and I'm going to Lemkin. I don't care *whose* nephew you are, who you know, whose dick you're sucking on. You're going *out*, I swear to you, you're going . . .

BAYLEN. Hey, fella, let's get this done . . .

ROMA. Anyone in this office lives on their *wits*. . . . (*to BAYLEN*) I'm going to be with you in a second. (*to WILLIAMSON*) What you're hired for is to *help* us—does that seem clear to you? To *help* us. *Not* to fuck us up . . . to help *men* who are going *out* there to try to earn a *living*. You *fairy*. You company man . . . I'll tell you something else. I hope you knocked the joint off, I can tell our friend here something might help him catch you. (*starts into the room*) You want to learn the first rule you'd know if you ever spent a day in your life . . . you never open your mouth till you know what the shot is. (*pause*) You fucking *child* . . . (*ROMA goes to the inner room, followed by BAYLEN.*)

LEVENE. You *are* a shithead, Williamson ... (*pause*)

WILLIAMSON. Mmm.

LEVENE. You can't think on your feet you should keep your mouth closed. (*pause*) You hear me? I'm *talking* to you. Do you hear me ... ?

WILLIAMSON. Yes. (*pause*) I hear you.

LEVENE. You can't learn that in an office. Eh? He's right. You have to learn it on the street. You can't *buy* that. You have to *live* it.

WILLIAMSON. Mmm.

LEVENE. *Yes.* "Mmm." *Yes. Precisely. Precisely.* 'Cause your partner *depends* on it. (*pause*) I'm *talking* to you, I'm trying to tell you something.

WILLIAMSON. You are?

LEVENE. Yes, I am.

WILLIAMSON. What are you trying to tell me?

LEVENE. What Roma's trying to tell you. What I told you yesterday. Why you don't belong in this business.

WILLIAMSON. Why I don't ...

LEVENE. You listen to me, someday you might say, "Hey ..." No, fuck that, you just listen what I'm going to say: your partner *depends* on you. You partner ... a man who's your "partner" *depends* on you ... you have to go *with* him and *for* him ... or you're shit, you're *shit*, you can't exist alone ...

WILLIAMSON. (*brushing past him*) Excuse me ...

LEVENE. ... excuse you, *nothing*, you be as cold as you want, but you just fucked a good man out of six thousand dollars and his goddamn bonus 'cause you didn't know the *shot*, if you can do that and you aren't man enough that it gets you, then I don't know what, if you can't take *some thing* from that ... (*blocking his way*) you're *scum*, you're fucking white-bread. You be as cold as you want. A *child* would know it, he's right.

(*pause*) You're going to make something up, be sure it will *help* or keep your mouth closed. (*pause*)

WILLIAMSON. Mmm. (*LEVENE lifts up his arm.*)

LEVENE. Now I'm done with you. (*pause*)

WILLIAMSON. How do you know I made it up?

LEVENE. (*pause*) What?

WILLIAMSON. How do you know I made it up?

LEVENE. What are you talking about?

WILLIAMSON. You said, "You don't make something up unless it's sure to help." (*pause*) How did you know that I made it up?

LEVENE. What are you talking about?

WILLIAMSON. I told the customer that his contract had gone to the bank.

LEVENE. Well, hadn't it?

WILLIAMSON. No. (*pause*) It hadn't.

LEVENE. Don't *fuck* with me, John, don't *fuck* with me . . . what are you saying?

WILLIAMSON. Well, I'm saying this, Shel: usually I take the contracts to the bank. Last night I didn't. How did you know that? One night in a year I left a contract on my desk. Nobody knew that but *you*. Now how did you know that? (*pause*) You want to talk to me, you want to talk to someone *else* . . . because this is *my* job. This is my job on the line, and you are going to *talk* to me. Now how did you know that contract was on my desk?

LEVENE. You're so full of shit.

WILLIAMSON. You robbed the office.

LEVENE. (*laughs*) Sure! I robbed the office. Sure.

WILLIAMSON. What'd you do with the leads? (*Pause. Points to the DETECTIVE's room.*) You want to go in there? I tell him what I know, he's going to dig up *something*. . . . You got an alibi last night? You better have one. What did you do with the leads? If you tell me what you did with the leads, we can talk.

LEVENE. I don't know what you are saying.

WILLIAMSON. If you tell me where the leads are, I won't turn you in. If you *don't*, I am going to tell the cop you stole them, Mitch and Murray will see that you go to jail. Believe me they will. Now, what did you do with the leads? I'm walking in that door — you have five seconds to tell me: or you are going to jail.

LEVENE. I . . .

WILLIAMSON. I don't care. You understand? *Where are the leads?* (*pause*) Alright. (*WILLIAMSON goes to open the office door.*)

LEVENE. I sold them to Jerry Graff.

WILLIAMSON. How much did you get for them? (*pause*) How much did you get for them?

LEVENE. Five thousand. I kept half.

WILLIAMSON. Who kept the other half? (*pause*)

LEVENE. Do I have to tell you? (*Pause. WILLIAMSON starts to open the door.*) Moss.

WILLIAMSON. *That* was easy, *wasn't* it? (*pause*)

LEVENE. It was his idea.

WILLIAMSON. *Was* it?

LEVENE. I . . . I'm sure he got more than the five, actually.

WILLIAMSON. Uh-huh?

LEVENE. He told me my share was twenty-five.

WILLIAMSON. Mmm.

LEVENE. Okay: I . . . look: I'm going to make it worth your while. I am. I turned this thing around. I closed the *old* stuff, I can do it again. *I'm* the one's going to close 'em. *I* am! *I* am! 'Cause I turned this thing a . . . I can do *that*, I dan do *anyth* . . . last night. I'm going to tell you, I was ready to Do the Dutch. Moss gets me, "Do this, we'll get well. ..." Why not. Big fuckin' deal. I'm halfway hoping to get caught. To put me out of my ... (*pause*) But it *taught* me something. What it taught me, that you've got to get *out* there. Big deal. So I wasn't cut out to be a thief. I was cut out to be a salesman. And now I'm back, and I got my *balls* back ... and, you know, John, you have the *advantage* on me now. Whatever it takes to make it right, we'll make it right. We're going to make it right.

WILLIAMSON. I want to tell you something, Shelly. You have a big mouth. (*pause*)

LEVENE. What?

WILLIAMSON. You've got a big mouth, and now I'm going to show you an even bigger one. (*starts toward the DETECTIVE's door*)

LEVENE. Where are you going, John? ... you can't do that, you don't want to do that ... hold, hold on ... hold on ... wait ... wait ... wait ... (*pulls money out of his pockets*) Wait ... uh, look ... (*starts splitting money*) Look, twelve, twenty, two, twen ... twenty-five hundred, it's ... take it. (*pause*) Take it all. ... (*pause*) Take it!

WILLIAMSON. No, I don't think so, Shel.

LEVENE. I ...

WILLIAMSON. No, I think I don't want your money. I think you fucked up my office. And I think you're going away.

LEVENE. I ... what? Are you, are you, that's why ... ? Are you nuts? I'm ... I'm going to *close* for you, I'm going to ... (*thrusting money at him*) Here, here, I'm going to *make* this office ... I'm going to be back there Number One. ... Hey, hey, hey! This is only the beginning. ... List ... list ... listen. Listen. Just one moment. List ... here's what ... here's what we're going to do. Twenty percent. I'm going to give you twenty percent of my sales. ... (*pause*) Twenty percent. (*pause*) For as long as I am with the firm. (*pause*) Fifty percent. (*pause*) You're going to be my partner. (*pause*) Fifty percent. Of all my sales.

WILLIAMSON. What sales?

LEVENE. What sales ... ? I just *closed* eighty-two *grand*. ... Are you fuckin' ... I'm *back* ... I'm *back*, this is only the beginning.

WILLIAMSON. Only the beginning ...

LEVENE. Abso ...

WILLIAMSON. Where have you been, Shelly? Bruce and Harriett Nyborg. Do you want to see the *memos* ... ? They're nuts ... they used to call in every week. When I was with Webb. And we were selling Arizona ... they're nuts ... did you see how they were *living*? How can you delude yours ...

LEVENE. I've got the check ...

WILLIAMSON. Forget it. Frame it. It's worthless. (*pause*)

LEVENE. The check's no good?

WILLIAMSON. You stick around I'll pull the memo for you. (*starts for the door*) I'm busy now ...

LEVENE. Their check's no good? They're nuts ... ?

WILLIAMSON. Call up the bank. *I* called them.

LEVENE. You did?

WILLIAMSON. I called them when we had the lead ... four months ago. (*pause*) The people are insane. They just like talking to salesmen. (*WILLIAMSON starts for door.*)

LEVENE. Don't.

WILLIAMSON. I'm sorry.

LEVENE. *Why*?

WILLIAMSON. Because I don't like you.

LEVENE. John: John: . . . my *daughter* . . .

WILLIAMSON. Fuck you. (*ROMA comes out of the DETECTIVE's door. WILLIAMSON goes in.*)

ROMA. (*to BAYLEN*) Asshole . . . (*to LEVENE*) Guy couldn't find his fuckin' couch the *living room* . . . Ah, Christ . . . what a day, what a day . . . I haven't even had a cup of *coffee*. . . . Jagoff John opens his mouth he blows my Cadillac. . . . (*sighs*) I swear . . . it's not a world of men . . . it's not a world of men, Machine . . . it's a world of clock watchers, bureaucrats, office-holders . . . what it is, it's a fucked-up world . . . there's no adventure *to* it. (*pause*) dying breed. Yes it is. (*pause*) We are the members of a dying breed. That's . . . that's . . . that's why we have to stick together. Shel: I want to talk to you. I've wanted to talk to you for some time. For a long time, actually. I said, "The Machine, there's a man I would work with. There's a man. . . ." You know? I never said a thing. I should have, don't know why I didn't. And that shit you were slinging on my guy today was *so* good . . . it . . . it was, and, excuse me, 'cause it isn't even my place to say it. It was admirable . . . it was the old stuff. Hey, I've been on a hot streak, so *what*? There's things that I could learn from you. You eat today?

LEVENE. Me.

ROMA. Yeah.

LEVENE. Mm.

ROMA. Well, you want to swing by the Chinks, watch me eat, we'll talk?

LEVENE. I think I'd better stay here for a while. (*BAYLEN sticks his head out of the room.*)

BAYLEN. Mr. *Levene* . . . ?

ROMA. You're done, come down and let's . . .

BAYLEN. Would you come in here, please?

ROMA. And let's put this together. Okay? Shel? Say okay. (*pause*)

LEVENE. (*softly to himself*) Huh.

BAYLEN. Mr. Levene, I think we have to talk.

ROMA. I'm going to the Chinks. You're done, come down, we're going to smoke a cigarette.

LEVENE. I . . .

BAYLEN. (*comes over*) . . . Get in the room.

ROMA. Hey, hey, hey, *easy* friend, That's the "Machine." That is Shelly "The Machine" Lev . . .

BAYLEN. Get in the goddamn room. (*BAYLEN starts manhandling SHELLY into the room.*)

LEVENE. Ricky, I . . .

ROMA. Okay, okay, I'll be at the resta . . .

LEVENE. Ricky . . .

BAYLEN. "Ricky" can't help you, pal.

LEVENE. . . . I only want to . . .

BAYLEN. Yeah. What do you want? You want to *what*? (*He pushes LEVENE into the room, closes the door behind him. Pause. ROMA starts adjusting his clothes preparatory to leaving the office. AARONOW enters.*)

AARONOW. Did they find the guy who broke into the office yet?

ROMA. No. *I* don't know. (*pause*)

AARONOW. Did the leads come in yet?

ROMA. No.

AARONOW. (*settling into a desk chair*) Oh, God, I hate this job.

ROMA. (*simultaneous with "job," exiting the office*) I'll be at the restaurant.

COSTUME PLOT

ACT I

LINGK:
Khaki slacks
Green sport coat
Plaid shirt
Tan tie
Brown belt
Wallabees (shoes)
Beige socks

WILLIAMSON:
Dk blue suit
White button dn
Blue silk tie
Back belt
Black Wing Tips
Navy socks

LEVENE:
Grey sharkskin suit
Lt blue shirt
Floral tie
Brown belt
Brown Wing Tips
Dk brown socks

MOSS:
Brown plaid
Peach shirt
Brn leather belt
Brown loafers
Rust brown socks

AARONOW:
Blue-Grey suit
Sweater vest
Lt blue shirt
Beige & blue tie
Black belt
Black Oxfords
Med Blue socks

ROMA:
Grey chalk stripe suit
White on white shirt
Red silk tie
Black slip-ons
Black belt
Black socks

ACT II

BAYLEN:
Blue blazer
Grey slacks
White shirt
Stripe tie
Black belt
Black Oxfords
Navy socks

LINGK:
Brown slacks
Lt green shirt
Car coat
Paisley tie

WILLIAMSON:
Blue stripe Oxford
Blue silk club tie

LEVENE:
Blue pinstripe
White shirt
Striped tie

MOSS:
Rain coat

AARONOW:
No vest
Med blue shirt
Blue striped tie

ROMA:
Pearl grey shirt
Blue silk tie

PROP LIST

ACT I

On stage:
2 Tables each with ashtrays and
2 Drinks with swizel sticks and cocktail napkins
  (one bourbon, one scotch.)

Upstage Right Booth Table:
Cruet of soy sauce
Salt & pepper shaker
Red napkin
Table advertisement

Prop Table:
Glass of wine with coctail napkin (Roma)
Gimlet with swizel stick and cocktail napkin (Lingk)
2 Chinese teacups (Moss & Aaronow)
Pair of chopsticks (Moss)
2 Red napkins (Moss & backup)
Briefcase (Aaronow)
Florida real estate map. (Roma)

ACT II

Prop Table:
Briefcase with legal pad and contract (Levene)
5 x 7 Pad (Baylen)
Ball point pen (Baylen)
Chicago Tribune (Aaronow)
Portfolio with five sets of forms, blue card attached
  to each. (Roma)
Pencils (Levene)
25 One dollar bills (Levene)
3 x 5 Cards (LEADS) (Williamson)

On Stage:
DS. of S.R. desk, Aaronows briefcase
On S.R. desk:
    Gold ashtray
    Pencils
    Dressing
On CS. desk:
    Gold ashtray
    loose papers
    Dressing
On coat tree S.L.:
    Moss' coat
    Aaronows coat
    Extra coat
    Umbrella
On coat tree shelves: Moss' briefcase and hat.
On D.L. chair; paper coffee cup and spiral note pad

Personal Props:

Roma:
Cigarette case with cigarettes
Lighter
Pen
Date book

Aaronow:
Lighter
Cigars

Williamson:
Lighter
Wallet
Pencil
Cigarettes

Levene:
Lighter
Cigars

Baylen:
Handcuffs in belt holder
Revolver in belt holster

Supplies:
Lime juice & club soda for Gimlet (Lingk)
Campari (Roma)
Butane
Lighter fluid
Coffee or tea
Water
Ice
Tissues
Colaring for drinks — coffee or carmel

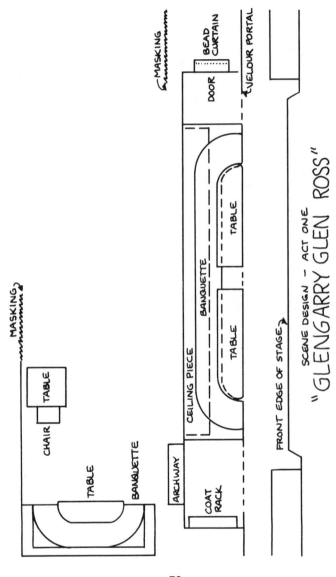

MASKING

TABLE

CHAIR

TABLE

BANQUETTE

MASKING

BEAD CURTAIN

DOOR

VELOUR PORTAL

CEILING PIECE

BANQUETTE

TABLE

TABLE

ARCHWAY

COAT RACK

FRONT EDGE OF STAGE

SCENE DESIGN — ACT ONE
"GLENGARRY GLEN ROSS"

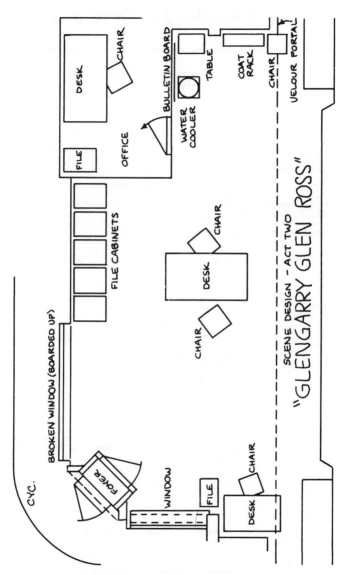

SCENE DESIGN - ACT TWO
"GLENGARRY GLEN ROSS"

Other Publications for Your Interest

HUSBANDRY

(LITTLE THEATRE—DRAMA)

By PATRICK TOVATT

2 men, 2 women—Interior

At its recent world premiere at the famed Actors Theatre of Louisville, this enticing new drama moved an audience of theatre professionals up off their seats and on to their feet to cheer. Mr. Tovatt has given us an insightful drama about what is happening to the small, family farm in America—and what this means for the future of the country. The scene is a farmhouse whose owners are on the verge of losing their farm. They are visited by their son and his wife, who live "only" eight hours' drive away. The son has a good job in the city, and his wife does, too. The son, Harry, is really put on the horns of a dilemma when he realizes that he is his folks' only hope. The old man can't go it alone anymore—and he needs his son. Pulling at him from the other side is his wife, who does not want to leave her job and uproot her family to become a farm wife. *Husbandry*, then, is ultimately about what it means to be a *husband*—both in the farm and in the family sense. *Variety* praised the "delicacy of Tovatt's dialogue", and called the play "a literate exploration of family responsibilities in a mobile society." Said *Time*: "The play simmers so gently for so long, as each potential confrontation is deflected with Chekhovian shrugs and silences, that when it boils into hostility it sears the audience." (#10169)

CLARA'S PLAY

(LITTLE THEATRE—DRAMA)

By JOHN OLIVE

3 men, 1 woman—Exterior

Clara, an aging spinster, lives alone in a remote farmhouse. She is the last surviving member of one of the area's most prominent families. It is summer, 1915. Enter an immigrant, feisty soul named Sverre looking for a few days' work before moving on. But Clara's farm needs more than just a few days' work, and Sverre stays on to help Clara fix up and run the farm. It soon becomes clear unscrupulous local businessmen are bilking Clara out of money and hope to gain control of her property. Sverre agrees to stay on to help Clara keep her family's property. "A story of determination, loyalty. It has more than a measure of love, of resignation, of humor and loyalty."—Chicago Sun-Times. "A playwright of unusual sensitivity in delineating character and exploring human relationships." —Chicago Tribune. "Gracefully-written, with a real sense of place."—Village Voice. A recent success both at Chicago's fine Wisdom Bridge Theatre and at the Great American Play Festival of the world-reknowned Actors Theatre of Louisville; and, on tour, starring Jean Stapleton. (#5076)

Other Publications for Your Interest

AGNES OF GOD
(LITTLE THEATRE—DRAMA)

By JOHN PIELMEIER

3 women—1 set (bare stage)

Doctor Martha Livingstone, a court-appointed psychiatrist, is asked to determine the sanity of a young nun accused of murdering her own baby. Mother Miriam Ruth, the nun's superior, seems bent on protecting Sister Agnes from the doctor, and Livingstone's suspicions are immediately aroused. In searching for solutions to various mysteries (who killed the baby? Who fathered the child?) Livingstone forces all three women, herself included, to face some harsh realities in their own lives, and to re-examine the meaning of faith and the commitment of love. "Riveting, powerful, electrifying new drama . . . three of the most magnificent performances you will see this year on any stage anywhere . . . the dialogue crackles."—Rex Reed, N.Y. Daily News. ". . . outstanding play . . . deals intelligently with questions of religion and psychology."—Mel Gussow, N.Y. Times. ". . . unquestionably blindingly theatrical . . . cleverly executed blood and guts evening in the theatre . . . three sensationally powered performances calculated to wring your withers."—Clive Barnes, N.Y. Post. (#236)

(Posters available)

COME BACK TO THE 5 & DIME, JIMMY DEAN, JIMMY DEAN
(ADVANCED GROUPS—DRAMA)

By ED GRACZYK

1 man, 8 women—Interior

In a small-town dime store in West Texas, the Disciples of James Dean gather for their twentieth reunion. Now a gaggle of middle-aged women, the Disciples were teenagers when Dean filmed "Giant" two decades ago in nearby Marfa. One of them, an extra in the film, has a child whom she says was conceived by Dean on the "Giant" set; the child is the Jimmy Dean of the title. The ladies' reminiscences mingle with flash-backs to their youth; then the arrival of a stunning and momentarily unrecognized woman sets off a series of confrontations that upset their self-deceptions and expose their well-hidden disappointments. "Full of homespun humor . . . surefire comic gems."—N.Y. Post. "Captures convincingly the atmosphere of the 1950s."—Women's Wear Daily. (#5147)

Other Publications for Your Interest

A WEEKEND NEAR MADISON
(LITTLE THEATRE—COMIC DRAMA)

By KATHLEEN TOLAN

2 men, 3 women—Interior

This recent hit from the famed Actors Theatre of Louisville, a terrific ensemble play about male-female relationships in the 80's, was praised by *Newsweek* as "warm, vital, glowing . . . full of wise ironies and unsentimental hopes". The story concerns a weekend reunion of old college friends now in their early thirties. The occasion is the visit of Vanessa, the queen bee of the group, who is now the leader of a lesbian/feminist rock band. Vanessa arrives at the home of an old friend who is now a psychiatrist hand in hand with her naif-like lover, who also plays in the band. Also on hand are the psychiatrist's wife, a novelist suffering from writer's block; and his brother, who was once Vanessa's lover and who still loves her. In the course of the weekend, Vanessa reveals that she and her lover desperately want to have a child—and she tries to persuade her former male lover to father it, not understanding that he might have some feelings about the whole thing. *Time Magazine* heard "the unmistakable cry of an infant hit . . . Playwright Tolan's work radiates promise and achievement." (#25051)

PASTORALE
(LITTLE THEATRE—COMEDY)

By DEBORAH EISENBERG

3 men, 4 women—Interior
(plus 1 or 2 bit parts and 3 optional extras)

"Deborah Eisenberg is one of the freshest and funniest voices in some seasons."—Newsweek. Somewhere out in the country Melanie has rented a house and in the living room she, her friend Rachel who came for a weekend but forgets to leave, and their school friend Steve (all in their mid-20s) spend nearly a year meandering through a mental landscape including such concerns as phobias, friendship, work, sex, slovenliness and epistemology. Other people happen by: Steve's young girlfriend Celia, the virtuous and annoying Edie, a man who Melanie has picked up in a bar, and a couple who appear during an intense conversation and observe the sofa is on fire. The lives of the three friends inevitably proceed and eventually draw them, the better prepared perhaps by their months on the sofa, in separate directions. "The most original, funniest new comic voice to be heard in New York theater since Beth Henley's 'Crimes of the Heart.'"—N.Y. Times. "A very funny, stylish comedy."—The New Yorker. "Wacky charm and wayward wit."—New York Magazine. "Delightful."—N.Y. Post. "Uproarious . . . the play is a world unto itself, and it spins."—N.Y. Sunday Times. (#18016)